# Dark Angelic Mills

# Dark Angelic Mills

Diane Pacitti

CANTERBURY
PRESS
Norwich

© Diane Pacitti 2020

First published in 2020 by the Canterbury Press Norwich
Editorial office
3rd Floor, Invicta House
108–114 Golden Lane
London EC1Y 0TG, UK
www.canterburypress.co.uk

Canterbury Press is an imprint of Hymns Ancient & Modern Ltd
(a registered charity)

Hymns Ancient & Modern® is a registered trademark of
Hymns Ancient & Modern Ltd
13A Hellesdon Park Road, Norwich,
Norfolk NR6 5DR, UK

The poem 'Before Pilate' appeared in *Third Way*, March 2016,
volume 40 number 2.

British Library Cataloguing in Publication data

A catalogue record for this book is available
from the British Library

978 1-78622-274-9

Typeset by Manila Typesetting Company

Printed and bound in Great Britain by
CPI Group (UK) Ltd

# Contents

# Foreword

*by the Rt Revd Rowan Williams*

These are poems that reflect the paradox of a building that is both central and marginal to the life of a complex city. We are invited to think about a history – and a present – in which the dominance of Anglican Christianity is not an obvious feature of the cultural landscape; and at the same time to recognize the ways in which the Cathedral holds memories and possibilities without which the city and the wider community could not thrive.

We are reminded of the bitterly compromised history of the Church itself, but also of the luminous perspective that faith still manages to bring to the world of work and stress and conflict and coexistence. It is appropriate that one of these poems is about fabric, about the dense weave of experience that makes the city what it is, with its history of textile-related industry. And another poem leaves us with the strong image of the building as a place of 'mutual standing / in the midst of the unknown'.

The presence of the Christian God is just such a 'standing in the midst', inviting mutual listening and understanding; and these poems finely draw out the way in which this vision and this confidence are to be rediscovered at the heart of the cathedral's vocation.

*The Rt Revd Rowan Williams*
*Master of Magdalene College, Cambridge,*
*and former Archbishop of Canterbury*

# Preface

Bradford Cathedral stands on a hill that was once grassy and a meeting-place of streams. Now it looks over a city punctuated by disused mills. The gold dome of a mosque crowns another hill. Close to the Cathedral is Kala Sangam, an intercultural arts centre sometimes used by the Cathedral for receptions. The view spread below includes areas of poverty and high unemployment. It is instantly clear that this environment is very different from the conventional idea of a 'cathedral city'.

As Poet in Residence during Bradford Cathedral's Centenary, I had the opportunity to explore this remarkable city in breadth and time-depth. My poem-sequence evokes the creation of the dales, introducing the presence of rock and water that will recur as the narrative unfolds. It tries to create a 'Godscape' which is destroyed by a version of the Fall, the Norman Conquest, which reduces land to ownership and monetary value.

Certain poems focus on significant moments of Bradford's history, such as the Civil War, the 2001 riots and the 'We are Bradford' response to the English Defence League. Others celebrate people who touched the life of Bradford and its landscape, from a working-class bell-ringer to Emily Bronte. People of today take their place alongside the northern saints depicted in the stained glass.

The poems recognize that Bradford's industrial wealth powered the Empire and contributed to our present ecological crisis. Its collapse, accompanied by demographic change, brought hardship, and also diversity and opportunities to what is now a city of faiths. Recognizing this, certain poems draw on practices and scriptural figures shared by Christianity and Islam. The Cathedral building holds communal history; its activities and liturgies provide a faithful rhythm of service and prayer. But it has had to develop a new role.

During the year, my conviction grew that a cathedral that has lost its former authority and works creatively with other faiths, seeing the 'Godself' in everyone, is living more truly the presence of Christ. I am convinced that if he was born today, Jesus would choose Bradford, rather than an ancient and wealthier cathedral city.

# Siting

Its task was present
When the site chose itself. Three streams or more
Which flowed together. A place of crossing.
A place to build a bridge,

To cluster homes.
The site was high enough
For a sweeping view of the dale, and yet the sky
Felt like a neighbour.

Then Bradford moved downhill. The streams
Flowed poison, and were culverted underground.
It seemed the church was stranded high and dry
In a new secular age.

Still in a city
Of crossed continents, thrown-together faiths,
Its purpose remains
To hold in prayer;

To work with all that is suppressed and choked
And bring it into light;
To site a crossing;
To sight hope.

# Genesis: Broade Ford

## 1 Godspan

Before one brick of this city could be laid,
Continents had to clash and be re-made.

In the beginning was no mind of man,
No human timescale, but a Godspan

Of transformation: age on age must plane
And gouge a landscape constantly made again.

Half-mile high, a glacial sheet must press
The rocks, and shape them under ice-stress.

Now let us watch, as tropical ferns are crushed
In a black layer, which is slowly pushed

To stretch out in a darkly sleeping seam
Under rock covers, holding in its dream

The exploding heat of industry, the fire
Which will fuel mills, will flare out in Empire.

Humans, whose ground was once an ocean-bed,
Make houses of sea-creatures long dead.

Pushed and piled by water, grains of sand
Weld in a building-stone which seams the land:

And bold Victorian constructs slice the sky.
Long, long before this, the Himalaya-high

Mountains of Scotland shrink, bit after bit
Swept down, to reach the dales as millstone grit.

And when the ice-melt torrented and bored,
It sculpted valleys, smoothed a river ford,

A broad ford in one particular dale,
Which gave a name to this city, and my tale,

Which has to flow like water, and take heed
Of sleeping fires, and chronicle human need,

And which, like its Cathedral, must embrace
All that is broken in one sheltering place.

## 2 Out of the Depths

Impossible for us, who are all rushing blood
And hammering heart, to begin to imagine the silence
Of that world of rock and water. Just as hard

To sense the stillness of a Yorkshire smothered
In the death-hug of ice, its surface seeming
To belong to an unknown planet. Then the flood

Crashing towards the sea, and the struggling emergence
Of tundra, out of which grow pine and birch,
And finally oak and ash. These progressions

Are so slow that they might well seem like stillness
And not change. And through it all,
Even when there was only colourless ice,

Or rock browns and greys, some nights the spot
That would become Bradford was transformed
To an oasis of silver, wiped to black

By a sudden cloud. And through this aeons-span,
Sunlight flowed in waves which ebbed to dark,
Like breathing slowed to the rhythm of the earth.

## 3 Chorus

Suddenly noises
squawks and breathy scurryings, and sharp
alarms, and mating-screams, and a forest-full
of beaks which sing the earth out of its sleep.

                     Suddenly the crash
and tusk-thrust of boar, and click of beetle,
and deer-bark and caterpillar-crawl
through the unheard swish of grass,

                 and elk, vole, starling
each throating out its life
               and the trout nudging
and nosing in its sealed river-world
of sound and vibration,
                noises threading
through undergrowth
            and rising through the air
that for so long was voiced by the wind alone.

Suddenly a bursting
of colours that are just as strong or seductive
as any sound
               yellow signalling loud
to butterfly, and tiger-stripe of bee,
and flash of blue in jay, and red slinking
lethal in fox.
             And slowly even leaf
becomes adventurous
            stretching out its spectrum
to the almost-yellow of a chestnut bud
enclosed in sticky red

             all this in a dale
that was once surly evergreen.

                              From dark spikes
and twisted trunk, the hawthorn reaches high
to refine itself into a spring of blossom
whose petals seem to be made of the air and light
they interrupt


                         yet somehow in the autumn
produces beaded red, passes through the guts
of thrushes with its seed
                              and loams the soil


                    in which fragile bird-skulls,
and the picked bones of rabbits slowly weld
with their hunters' remains, bed with the forest's
abandonment of leaf,


                              all in a slow
economy of exchange that grows from rock
and insistent water.


                         And from time to time,
Groups of humans waded through the river
Into pathless grass, navigating by the sun,
And disappeared through the dale as if they had broken
Into someone else's dream.

## 4 Church

Nobody knows when it disappeared. No chronicle
Speaks of axe and flames, or even of the slow
Tear of wind, the arrow-attack of rain
On that high exposed spot. We have no knowledge
Of the settlement it served, or the date it first
Crouched low upon the hill-top, swathed in sky;
But whether it was bodied in sawn trunk,
Or wattled twigs,

           the worshippers must have thought
Their lives had paused in a deep forest clearing.
That space was human-sized. It left no records
For historians to labour, and no walls
For costly maintenance. At an unknown time,
It gave its toll of wood back to the earth,
Surrendered all its broken stone to the hill.

Because yes, there was stone. Outside, a cross
Whose habitat was weather, grass and sky.
The Saxons took a torture-instrument
And filled its stark arms with flowing curves,
With generous linking forms. All that is left
Is one broken fragment, quietly placed
Inside the Cathedral.

           If you look quickly,
You just might see in its shape a wrist broadening
To a hand which is closed, perhaps to clasp
Another unseen hand. Within it flow
Those intricate linked curves. It reaches to us
From its lost date, reaches through a second church
Burnt by Scots raiders, reaches out of the horror
Of a Roman death-tool, to assert 'I am
Connectedness. I am the flow of life.'

## 5 Domesday

*Taxable units: 15 total.*
*Tax assessed: 15 geld units.*
*Value to lord in 1066: £4.*

Black smouldering fields: number unknown,
The Conqueror pushes north along the Aire,
Plundering, burning crops on either side.

Burnt houses: number unknown.
Death count: first chronicled figure:
100,000, which historians doubt.
Genocide?
The use of this term
Is being debated thoughtfully by scholars.
But precise death-statistics do not trouble
The foreign soldiers as they round up sheep.
Mass starvation is the planned consequence
Of the laying waste of the North.

Policy of retribution:
100% successful, judged against
Objective set: a subjugated North.

*Ploughlands: 8.*
*Woodland: 0.5 leagues.*
*Lord in 1066: Gamal son of Barth.*

Broade Ford, lately seized from the Saxon Gamal,
Of high taxable value, a convenient
Payback gift to one of the Conqueror's men.
Match found: neither low nor too high-ranked,
In Ilbert, placed as a surveillance tool.
The regime needs Norman eyes everywhere.

Always the occupying army first,
And then the bureaucrats. Soon an assessor
Arrives at Broade Ford. His Domesday brief
Is tax, profit, ownership. He casts his eye
On what we have seen as river, hawthorn, jay,
And Godspace. He writes his entry
In admin-format, with punctilious hand.

*Ilbert has it. It is waste.*

# I Come From . . .

*A tribute to Aleena, Saariyah, Chloe, Nida and Iqra, five Bradford schoolgirls whose 'I Come From' poem featured in the BBC television event 'We Are Bradford'.*

I come from forest oaks
and bruising weights of Yorkshire rock. I come
from a craftsman's chisel.

I come from the dung-clotted straw
of a stable. I come from dirty feet
washed by my founder just before he died.

I come from an empire
that wrote its will across a tiny kingdom.
I come from a far land, across deserts
and seething seas.
I come from closer than your skin: I come
from a longing deep within you.

I come from Judas.
I come from the Crusades, and countless acts
that betray my founder.
I come from a king's wish to divorce his wife.

I come from the footsteps
of unknown people. I come from stories
that will never be told.

I come from a parched wilderness
in which a man struggled for forty days;
I come from bare concrete. I come
from the cries of the marginalised.

I come from the taste of wine, and I have known it
turn into vinegar.

I come from the ultimate failed project.
Followers fleeing; leader put to death.
A management disaster. The twist is:
the project didn't die.

I come bloodied
by the deaths of martyrs. I come grounded
in day-to-day acts. I come floating
on the silence of eternity.

I come from Bradford.
I come from the grit and courage of its people.
I come from unbounded Spirit
which I anchor
firm in the midst of shops and concrete, firm
and deep in this city's heart.

# To Any Visitor

Welcome here. Perhaps your visit is squashed
Between shopping, other sights. But you have arrived,
And you walk through time. Above your head is wood
That three centuries ago stood forest-thick.

It is thought those rough stones that wall the nave
Are part of an earlier church which raiders destroyed;
The story told by this place will help you to turn
Your failures into the building-blocks of yourself.

Do not be deterred by the glassy-robed brilliance
Of the saints who line the walls: like you they knew
The dark places. Do not shrink from the perfect
Marble of the monuments: they might mark

The grief of a dead child, or a life sounding out
In surprising ways, like the trumpeter who played
At Waterloo. Here drawn in glass are the figures
Of local men who suffered the Great War.

Here is a hospitality which contains
The dead and the living. This place might ring with debate,
Or provoke with art. It is here that homeless people
Come to be warmed by companionship and food.

The Child who was laid in an animal trough has a way
Of finding just enough space. Choose a corner, a chair,
To take the pulse of your life and feel it connect
With a larger energy, rest on a deeper silence.

The infinity that is God is able to fit
Into just enough time. A moment is long enough
To change from tourist to pilgrim. Journey on.
Let what you see connect with your life's travel.

Yours: faithfully. This church held the world
Of your far-distant ancestors in its prayers:
Become part of that prayer, then take it outside
Into the driven crowds, the impatient roads.

# St Peter's Church

*Until 1919, Bradford Cathedral was the parish church
of St Peter.*

Drop the 'saint' for a moment. Come to think of it,
drop even the name. Jesus wasn't one
to make bad jokes, but calling him a rock?
Any church built on him would slide
and shift on sand. He'd happily go back
to simple Simon.

Yet once he tried to make a sort-of-church;
three stone huts to wall in that moment
of mountain-top
rather as you'd hope to trap
a breathed-in rose whose crimson sings summer
in a tiny scent-flask.

And since he'd seen a sky-ful of light streaming
from one man, why would he let it shrink
down to the candle-flames
of three memories?
And why did Jesus set off so soon?
Always that road.

Why couldn't Jesus wrap that light-memory
around himself and hug it close like a robe?
Why couldn't he reward
his three friends, and even himself,
for just one moment?

Drunk on light, Peter stumbled
down and down
to town-stink and resentments, to the people
clawing at Jesus, to his friends failing
yet again. Sucked down and down
to that sick Passover

running with the blood of God's own first-born,
while the oppressor and his line went free.
Gloating. Sucked down
to the shit of his own self:
heroics turned to panic, boasts to self
preservation.

Now Mount Tabor
is crowned by a church with gold and alabaster.
At its foot, a shop. Coach-loads of pilgrims
pass those unbuilt huts. But this is not
Saint Peter's church. So how
might that be recognised?

Shifting sands
solidifying in rock, as in the stone
which walls this cathedral. Hope persisting
in the face of a hopeless past.
A journeying
of fallible people. Something unseen.

A treading
of glory-glimpses, light-epiphanies
out to the stoniest road,
the most hostile soil,
which does not trample out that light but scatters
its live sparks like seeds.

# Choral Evensong:
# His Bright Materials

The Parish Room: a hatch with sandwiches, juice;
Tables squared for a meeting. On the wall
The carers' quilt, each sewn square a postcard
From a circumscribed life. The noisy eruption

Of boys straight from school; the rushing-around
Of sloganed tee, striped ties, brave pair of shorts
Worn in the cold. Boys of varying ages,
Skin colours, heights. Excitement when a greyhound

Appears at the door, seeming to leap straight
From a tapestry, from a far more ancient world
Than the tune thumped on the piano, or the mobile
Addressed in Polish. On to rehearsal room.

Here we are backstage, and it can be difficult
To step into performance. A child is struggling
With the fastenings of his robe. Sung Yorkshire vowels
Persist; some boys produce an invented language

Their director calls Singerese. With skill he negotiates
Offside remarks, lapses, forgotten scores;
Cajoles and leads. A - seventeenth-century liturgy
Is rehearsed in bite-sized chunks. Sung demonstration.

Repeat. Repeat. A boy's sheet music drifts
Down to the floor. They reach the Amens.
Just across the close, the dark is at work
On the stained glass, watering down colours,

Weakening shapes. A priest is preparing to hold
The world in prayer, which will happen whether or not
The chairs are empty, whether or not the world
Even cares. And this prayer will burst into song.

# Choral Evensong

Human life
Seemed to Bede of Northumbria like a sparrow
Flying from the dark
Through the length of a fire-lit hall

Then back into stormy dark.
But now at nightfall
In this dim pillared space, I rather feel
How in the midst of invading dark, we weave

A fabric of sound;
How in the shelter
Of a brief moment, which might collapse
Into sickness or worse,

We dare to sing;
How even though the choristers' red robes
Are rain-dashed from a January storm,
They move in slow procession,

Down the aisle
Passing heavy walls which hold the dead:
Then a man's voice
Sings out a phrase which winds a path through the dark

Silence. Other mouths make
An inroad through the emptiness, sing Glory;
Even as they voice
Our vulnerability, as they implore,

'Make haste to help us.' And now the perils
Of this night close in, as we admit the dark
Of human failure.
Only this way

Can we enter Mary's Song,
Which grows out of a seed of light planted
Deep in the dark of a woman's body, planted
In the night of Roman rule.

And the shell of the nave
Is bodied with sound, as if it existed
Only to be a vessel overflowing
With light made audible;

As if its emptiness
Existed only to become a womb
Of swelling sound, of a radiance translated
Into sung word

And the silence which defines it.
Not Bede's straight journey
From dark to dark, but rather a mutual standing
In the midst of the unknown, a shared longing

To voice the sacred in a fragile moment;
And even more miraculous, some of us strive
To perfect that singing,
So that every phrase

Seems to live on
In the heart
Of the dark
Into which it disappears.

# Northerner

Always they could place him
By that accent, and of course the town he came from
Was a bit of a local joke. When he reached the capital,
The braying elite made it absolutely clear
He'd never be Premier League.
                                    And yet he carried
The North with him: even in the din
Of that metropolis he gave out a silence
That belonged to the rock-strewn hills and the deep
Dales.
                                    And he knew just how hard
Northern people work: how women labour
To produce cloth, how keeping sheep
Can be an absolute pain, how bosses screw
The last ounce out of you. He put this stuff
In his stories, while the big literary noises
Of the Empire penned their elegant thoughts on war
Or the upper crust. And people listened to him;
They even remembered.
                                    But don't get me wrong,
He was earthy all right: he could offend.
And between you and me, he was far too matey
With the wrong sort.
                                    That capital in the south
Thought it had shut him up. But afterwards,
He visited his friends, caged up in fear,
In a maze prison of streets. He knew at once
He had to get them out. In fact, he had better
Lead the way, because this fierce squabble
Of trade and shoppers, these crowds whose cheer
Mutated mid-sound in their gaping mouths
To an execution-roar,

                              this city hooked
On toxic power games: this was no place
To spend your resurrection. Somewhere at the edge
Of his mind a bird-trill, a warbler's churr,
Water was plashing in that narrow street;
The sky became big. Now stones were crunching
Under his pierced feet that the lake would wash
With its own tender rhythms. He was home.

# Clay Genesis

I used to think
How the potter's will shaped
The boggy clay: how its lifeless lump received
The maker's sudden impulses, the push

Of hand, the dent of thumb;
But now I watch
The maker close her eyes
To feel for the shape

As if it was always there,
As if when God
Worked with earth dust
He could feel the buried life,

And some dynamic in the clay impelled him
To uncurl the embryo form,
And flesh the limbs
Which started to assert

Their muscled reach;
So that between the maker
And thing-being-made there slowly grew a pull
And counter-tug, a seesaw of creating,

Which quivered to a balance, and from this
A human form emerged.
And then I think
Of Michelangelo's God

Withdrawing slowly
From the vulnerable,
And just-made human, right to that last frail touch
Of fingertip, which lingers

Even as it pulls
Away. The potter stands
Back, and sees that it is very
Good, but it has passed from her.

The new creature
Looks wonderingly around, already living
The terror and the joy
Of being herself.

# A Bradford Christmas

There have to be shepherds
in this former hub of wool; there must be sheep,
not just that carved beast at Waterstones;

Out in dark dales
we glimpse a few white blurs, soft woolly shapes
penned in by dry stone walls. No sign of shepherds.
Of course, they are watching Netflix, surrounded
by secular Christmas cards.

People from the east
have already arrived, bringing their knowledge
and other precious gifts. Gold gleams in the dome
of the Grand Mosque. Even old Yorkshire shops
stock unfamiliar spices;

The ten year census
has been returned; the City Hall computers
seethe with statistics.

                              The Home Office
is sure some immigrant has slipped the net,
perhaps a minor. Following a lead,
an inspector bursts into an outbuilding,
and finds a rag and bone horse.

A peanut advert
appears in Broadway with a no-nonsense message:
'Wise men don't come bearing bruschetta'.

Excited children
wear flashing reindeer antlers, and the god
of the pagan mid-winter, fat-bulging
and red-cheeked, is holding noisy court
at this consumption-fest,

                              is holding court
at crammed pubs, at fully booked hotels.
Festive laughter leaks from each lit window
into the cold night.

The streets empty.
A homeless man chooses a half-safe spot
behind a dustbin.

And a woman lies in bed
pondering how she has just been told that Christ
is born in our hearts, is born anywhere:

and the whole sprawling city seems to tremble
on the brink of change
as if the very stones

of proud carved walls
long to revert to rock, collapse to a cave
that might offer shelter.

And this sleeping hub of shops and homes and dreams
flitting through minds begins to feel like a sound
struggling in the throat,

like a half-formed word
longing to be uttered,
like a deed

waiting to birth in the hands and feet and flesh
of just one Bradford person,
waiting still

hidden in a womb of dark to speak out

with the clarity of love

# Here

If you have arrived

                       laden with baggage,
Tired and confused, because your reasoning led you
To the wrong destination, and you were like
The Magi who went first to Herod's palace
And not to this poor place;

                    Or if perhaps the surprise
Sneaked up behind, as you were buckling down
To a life at best boring, like the shepherds
In their cold field, staring at a humdrum sky
Which suddenly streamed light;

                    Or perhaps, like Joseph,
You have been pulled into something you did not choose
And cannot quite disown. Or perhaps you function
As a puzzled extra, like the oxen, witnessing
The convulsions of a birth,

                    But it scarcely matters
What route you travelled, now that you are here
In this draughty stable, here with the smell of dung
And you can see the child,

                    And whether you claim
To have a faith or none, you have reached a place
Where words like 'belief' and 'faith' dissolve
And re-make themselves, as you draw close to the baby
Vulnerable in the dirt,

and those tiny hands
Disarm your ideas of power, and God.
This dark obscure place is where the world
Might be transformed, and here you receive

Something new of yourself.

# Birthing Place

*A poem for Bradford's Marie Curie Hospice, and the Cathedral's Lights to Remember service.*

Where can we find the Child? We are certain to find him
In Bethlehem now, in a slum without water,
In the shadow of the Wall.

                      Or perhaps the new family
Fled their Syrian home when the Herod-roar
Of artillery drew close.

                      If a few years ago
We had visited Calais, and seen the crushed cardboard
Of a box that had been a cot, it might not have told us
We had only just missed him.

                      We need to search:
But here in a hospice? What can be new-born
In a place reserved for the dying?

                      To discover this
We have to make the angels come down from the sky
And put on nurse uniforms to engage
With the messiness of flesh;

                      Now, in this place
Removed from our usual comforts, we need to add
Visitors, each one bearing the gift
Of love and grief.

We must make the wise men
Forget their book-learning, sky-knowledge
And bend the knee to frailty.


Because at the very
Centre is a vulnerable body
Held safely: here a unique self
Is still being birthed.


And here in the nave,
The Bethlehem star is refracting into two hundred
Candle-flames each carrying a name,
Each bringing forth a life.

# A Divided Place?

Bradford is helpless. An army waits outside:
Tomorrow they will massacre, loot and smash.
Their commander has it in for those hate preachers
Who turn their sacred text like a gun on the state,

And on every pleasure. England is split
In two. Bloody clashes in the south, the north.
Each side attacks with words, which can disfigure
Your enemy just as effectively as bullets,

Can make him less than human, or enlarge him
To terrifyingly more. Violent mobs control
London; its fanatic sects are a threat
To order. The head of the state seems lost.

It is 1643. The British Isles
Are fragmenting. Scotland started this,
And now pulls two ways. Wales, Ireland seethe
With armed men and anger. Europe watches.

So what happened to Bradford? The commander said
A spirit-woman in white pleaded that night,
'Pity poor Bradford.' Then his force plundered,
But spared lives. Other cities weren't so lucky.

**2**

An angry narrative: now let us stay
In that turbulent seventeenth century, and tell
A different story.

                              Let us seek a calm
Room in Bradford, threatened from outside
But still within. Now let us be aware
Of our plain dress, and enter a silence
That breathes peace, that patiently prepares
To live the day of small things. We are here
With Yorkshire folk: in their transparent world
There are no oaths, no doffing of the hat
To wealth and power. They call themselves Friends.

Far to the south, a striking of spades
On dry soil. A group of landless men
Lay claim to a patch of land. A northern voice
Attacks the 'Norman yoke', which took the earth
From those who labour it, which used the sword
To carve out chunks of England. If we stay
With this band of Diggers, we will be scoured
By winds, wrung weak with toil, and finally driven
Away by swords;

                         and yet that hope persists
In Africa, Asia, in all colonised lands,
That the earth might be a common treasury, shared
By all who live and work it.

Now a cacophony
Of voices, rising as they learn to speak
For the first time: foot-soldiers claim a vote
For 'the poorest man in England'; women wear
White ribbons for peace, and take their cause
To Parliament; they dare to act alone.

That northern weaver claims education
As a universal right.

                                    This is an England
That has tried and killed its king; this is a world
Turned upside down, and so the voices rise
Visionary, full of hope, sometimes unhinged,
And sometimes reaching straight out to us:

And as the land painfully re-makes itself,
It is from the neglected north, the west,
The land's 'dark corners', economically slow,
That prophetic voices come,

                              And base their visions
On the very sacred texts that others scour
For harsh judgements. These new voices call
On Christ the friend of the marginalised and poor;
Christ who transforms this world, Christ who will rise
In his sons and daughters.

                              Now let us return
To a calm space in Bradford, to a stillness
Of people not all white, or labourers' brown.
We might be in a meeting-place, church, mosque,
Temple or synagogue; let us hear the hum
Of community being built in sports-field, school,
In drop-in place and refuge. Here we live
That second narrative.

**3**

> But a noise
Is jarring from the streets; the smell of smoke,
A thousand Muslims gathered as a book
Flames and smoulders outside City Hall.
This is thirty years ago, but that fault-line
Does not go away. And twelve years on,
The fire is spreading: flare of petrol bombs,
Blaze of a club, a pub, the choking fumes
Of torched cars, all fanned by rumour
And fierce grievance.

> Large vehicles wait
At the city's edge with police armed for riot
And then go in. A night of youthful fury
Sentenced, named as 'riot against the Crown'.
It writes off years of youth for Muslim men
In prison.

> The whole country stares
And shuffles awkwardly, not wanting
To see its image in a city called
'A racial tinderbox', a place whose riots
Are the worst for twenty years upon this mainland;
Its segregation judged the most severe.
Just google 'riot' and the city's name
Is high in the hits. So what will happen
To Bradford now? A nervous England watches.

**4**

We are Bradford: we are a police
Who have stood petrol bombs, who have held in place
The hate-inciters, and devised a strategy
That other cities will copy.

We are Bradford: and we refuse
To hand our story over to outsiders;
Whether they are a hallowed search engine,
The media, or the English Defence League
Who call us 'the big one' and today
Are arriving in our city.

                                 We are Bradford:
We are Women for Peace; we will fill this city
With our green ribbons.

                                 We are Bradford:
We are a young Muslim man who has chosen
To stay away, to not be provoked.

We are Bradford: especially we are
A man who has just been spat at, 'Muslim bomber',
And now is clenching his fists against his side,
Shaking.

                             We are the Bradford
That the media label 'white working class',
We don't want these outsiders causing trouble.

We are Bradford: we are a shopper
Who treated this like any other Saturday
And is now rushing from a hurled bottle.

'We are Bradford': we are a movement
City-wide, a coming together
In a peace event, to set against the fury
Of the pent-up invaders.

                              We are Bradford:
We are a Cathedral dean who moves across
The space they have just vacated, using rosemary
To sprinkle water, ritually expelling
The presence of hate.

                    And the other faiths approve
Because we are Bradford.

**5**

                              When a city decides
To write its own story, it is never
Just one act. And yet a community joined
In an act of shared creation points the way
To narratives of hope which begin to sketch
Tentative outlines over the blank pages
Of the city's future, and we look again
With different eyes at chapters that seemed closed.
So that in front and even far behind us,
The landscape is changed.

                              You find one story
Written all over the city in pilasters
And fluted columns, fleshed out in cherubs,
Picked out in classical swags. This is the story
Of Britain's claim to be the second Rome;
It tells of a Bradford smirched with mills,
Wool capital of the world, part of an empire
Which wrote its will in red across the globe.
This powerful story chooses not to depict
Its dark shadow-side of conquered peoples,
At whom the Bible was too often pointed
Like a gun, tool of a conquering mission,
Not shared as a book of peace.

If we ascend
To Little Germany now, there is buddleia straggling
On a listed building, seeming less alive

Than the plumped-out roses carved in stone below.
A dark slit that was a letter-box
Gapes into vast-roomed emptiness.

If we raise our eyes
Past the pilasters, high to the green dome
Of the 'Methodist Cathedral of the North',
We see a restored façade: behind are flats;
Below, unlet shops, a skin parlour.

If we go to Kirkgate,
Stately walls still speak of Pearl Assurance.
Below: pink price-tags, cut-price pillows.
Not long ago the Council objected
To a 'garish' shop-sign.

If we travel east
To Bradford Moor, and see a schoolgirl running
To greet her friend, the odds make it likely
At least one of the girls comes from a family
Which struggles to feed her.

We do not need to visit
A job centre; the press has already told us
That Britain's youngest city cannot offer
Sufficient work to its young.

              But Bradford was never
Free of poverty: when the industrialists carved
Their status in crests, the workers huddled
Low in the blackened city; families fitted
In hutch-dark back-to-backs. And always
There was a second tale, a counter-flow
To the imperial narrative. Out of struggle
The people improvised with penny banks
Building societies; they formed the co-op.
Names that now sound institutional
Were radical experiments. In Leeds Road
A blown-up banner speaks of the Commonweal,
Proclaims the Independent Labour Party, birthed
By a Manningham strike.

                              That banner still refracts
Into home-made slogans, chanted cries;
Into chalked pavements, and the human chain
Stretching to 'Hug the Odeon'; into tents
By 'Westfailed' or 'Wastefield', once the city's
Hole in the heart. The tramp of marching feet
Echoes through Bradford: unions, suffragettes,
Through to Muslim children schooled in their rights
Marching to City Hall. And still this city
Improvises, cares: late at weekends
A team takes to the streets, spreads out to assist
Drink-dazed clubbers, calm aggressive pubbers,
Protect the harried homeless. Volunteers
Hi vis and yellow-vested, minister here
As Street Angels.

                                                        It is a city
Of faiths, and faith.

**6**

                                         Come with me
To a Bradford-wide conversation, sparked
By literature: we are near the Festival's end.
Come with me into the ancient space
Of the Cathedral; come with me to hear
A Sufi poem, and a Hindu chant,
A gospel hymn, each weaving its bright strand
Of words and sound in a many-textured prayer,
A shared meditation,

                                    Which now tells
A story acting as a counter-flow
To the imperial tale which was set in stone
When craftsmen hewed and carved a Wool Exchange
Like a Venetian palace.

                               This other story
Draws those who were once subject in the Empire
Centre-stage; it must also serve the descendants
Of those who worked the mills, the Empire's drudges;
Its diverse citizens must each feel
'We are Bradford' in a narrative driven
By small significant acts. Sometimes this story
Struggles to be heard as the city faces
An uncertain future, wearing scars
And burn-marks from the past. Yet this year
The BBC empowered Bradford voices
To speak it out loud.

                              Whenever it is faithful
As a place of refuge; whenever it faces
Hardship with its characteristic grit,
Using that hardship as material
From which to create; whenever its people
Come together, but still respect
The neighbourhood of difference, then this story
Is Bradford.

# Women for Peace

*Women for Peace was part of Bradford's response to a rally of
the English Defence League in 2011.*

Once upon a time
green branched and leafed and interwove
in the midst of concrete;

Once upon a time
Bradford taxi drivers flew green ribbons,
each one a roving ambassador
for the republic of peace;

Once upon a time
the hate-makers burst from the Interchange
with shouts and war-chants, and they were met
with song;

Once upon a time
Muslim women twinned with Christian; voices
twining and soaring: the extravagance of hope
set against caging hate.

The time is now. The voices are always here
but you did not listen. You let your ears be blasted
by certain leaders. You did not see
the green bursting out of sterile stone:
you were blinded by your screens.

                                    The song is here.
This is no story-book tale: this is a history
which could be the future.

# Mary / Maryam

You might call
on one of these women as she sits alone
holding deep within her heart the wonder
of her son's birth.

You might watch the other
tell a puzzled priest how God's giving
is infinite, beyond human counting.

Then you might surround Mary with silence,
and wait for Maryam's prayer to speak loud
but that would be too simple.

Open your ears: hear Mary's great outpouring
of prophecy; listen as she voices
the longings of her people, as she speaks
a new world into being, as if it were
already here, God's justice overturning
the hierarchies of power:

Open your eyes to Maryam, an example
for all who withdraw from wounding tongues
and mob judgements, all who shed
the clamorous needs of self, all who encounter
the mystery that is God with silent hearts.

To visit either of these women
is to be surprised; it is to suspend
our mean assessment of what life might be:

Maryam praying
in a winter-cold sanctuary, surrounded
by ripe scents, by swelling summer fruits;

Mary in a place of dirty straw
watching as the dull light curves and glitters
around three gifts from the east.

Mary's whole being turned to a vessel
in which God can grow;

                              Maryam holding
a son only just emerged from her womb,
a solely human baby who is granted
God-utterance, who through his tiny lips
protects the one whose flesh encircled him
and held him safe;

both are brushed
by the breath of angels; both forced to tread
the dragging weight of earth:

Maryam giving birth
alone in the rocky desert, Mary gripped
by labour-pangs in a place of cattle-dung,
then forced to flee abroad.

The threat of stoning
hangs over both.

Mary brimming
with mother-joy, yet told at the same moment,
'A sword shall pierce your soul.' Maryam lamenting
'Would I had died before this and was a thing
forgotten';

The two women
mirror each other, step aside to difference,
and quietly interchange;

One woman
through whom two faiths that have vilified and fought
can exchange gifts.

# St Cuthbert Visits the Mirror Pool

I

He had hardly known glass in his life, just the odd tiny bead,
and here he was trapped like a living fish in ice
inside this Victorian window, given skin
of an indoor pallor, smothered in the bishop's robes
he had tried to reject in life. Tenderly, he laid down
the crowned head they had placed in the crook of his arm
for saint-spotting nerds. His dear friend Oswald
had no need of body-parts now. He forced himself
from the clinging glass, which closed back on his shape,
leaving him free to wander through a place
where heavy slabs of black were interspersed
with arcaded dimness.

It felt like a blown-up
version of his Durham tomb: elaborate, prayerful,
but too enclosing. All his life he had searched
for a different sacredness. With his own hands,
he had built his prayer-cell: walls of rough stone
and claggy mud, a ceiling of sky.
To see that sky he gladly would have burst
out of the turret, but he chose to step
through the porch door, to follow a long trail
of bare and poorly shod and well-heeled feet.

His own feet barely recognised
the tamed grass; even his friends the stars,
who used to pray with him through the long nights,
were dulled by the muzzy air. A strangely smooth
and grass-less highway edged by fortresses
beckoned him down into a shock of space,

an almost-circle that no rock had levelled
or river gouged. And within it a trinity
of bowls cupped to the sky. Truly he had stumbled
on a holy place. The saint who used to pray
waist-high in sea all night now stood alone
in the dry heart of the city, sensing water.

**2**

He couldn't place that animal. Otter-dark,
and almost with seal's eyes. Utterly unlike
any cur he had known. Restrained by a lead
like an untamed horse, yet meek. Inside this circle
everything was strange. First a stream of mist
rolled straight at him, yet he was not wet.
This was indeed a place of miracles.
But no, he summoned from his human life
the sky-splitting wings of the eider duck,
or an otter's lithe furriness as it rubbed
his sea-chilled feet; these things were no less wonders
than a targeted burst of mist.

                       And now this creature
straining at him, her tail beating the air
in joyous percussion, while her owner,
tried to tap life out of a hand-held stone,
then glanced up, and reduced the saint to air.
A sharp tug of the lead, and the animal
left with his secret. Then water flowed.
True, it was shallow, but it held in its mirror
an infinity of sky. He was content.

The people came.
And at the same time, on the edge of his sensing,
a threatening hum, an endless rotation
of closed chariots which flashed like swords,
with faces trapped inside. This was a circle
of restlessly revolving souls who glimpsed
but could not reach this inner place of joy.
For so he found it: here the people wore
unearthly colours, quite unlike the browns
and coarse cloth he had known. Here children plentiful
as Biblical fish sent water splashing through him
with a shriek of spray, while giant-sized adults laughed
and basked and let their Saturday morning float
on the wonder of water.

The paler-skinned
were scantily clad, suggesting harsh need,
and yet were sturdily fleshed. But who were these?
Dark-skinned, with flowing robes and draped veils?
Were these the people of the scriptures: prophets,
apostles, holy women, come to meet
with living folk, jointly to build the kingdom
of heaven here on earth, here in this place?

Then Cuthbert understood; now he could sense
currents of deep pain in all these beings,
and ebb-tides of loss. His heart went out
to each fellow-human. He let his mind
enlarge itself around an astonishing fact:
that people of such various skins and countries
should meet in this remote and often-chill
realm of Northumbria, meet not to fight
or even to barter, but to join in play.
The saint of the north stood almost to his calves
in Council water, drinking in wonders.

# A Prayer to St Hilda

Brexit-divided, internet-obsessed,
Mobile-myopic, helplessly in thrall
To bought stuff, we cry across a gulf:
Saint of wise love, it is to you we call.

Calm woman who held power in an age
When the sword ruled: to slash, cut down, enthral,
And used that power to build and reconcile,
Help us to build a sheltering home for all.

Latin-literate royal, who drew inside
A herdsman from the silent field and stall,
Moved by his soaring Saxon hymn to God:
Saint of wise love, it is to you we call.

Host of the Synod, who found yourself
On the losing side, yet felt an inner call
To stay with the victors, and to reconcile,
Help us to build a sheltering home for all.

Mother of Whitby, strong Abbess of nuns
And, daringly, monks as well, your realm a small
Cluster of homes, of worship, work, and care:
Saint of wise love, it is to you we call.

Of course, we idealise you, but you faced
Cruel cold and failure, prejudice, and the gall
Of bodily pain, and out of that you built:
May we create a sheltering home for all.

Saint, pray for us, as wealth appreciates
Itself, as poverty deepens, as we bawl
Across this gulf at faces we don't see:
Saint of wise love, it is to you we call.

Help us to sing in unexpected tongues;
Help us to welcome in the marginal;
Heal our divisions; make us whole,
That we may be a sheltering home for all.

Transform each barrier wall into the tall
Support of a broad tent, a spacious hall:
Saint of wise love, it is to you we call;
Help us to build a sheltering home for all.

# Walking the Cathedral Textiles

*A tribute to Polly Meynell, who designed these textiles.*

It is a century
since the Great War ended. Around the altar, blood
red cloths confront me. Dark horizontals
run across their flat terrain like rows
of men, barbed wire, munitions. Underground
stretch long trenches.

A huge globe of a moon
lights the stuck lines.

With these shapes imprinted
deep in my mind, I walk through the city,
through a dark grid of streets, past gaunt verticals
of industrial chimneys. Here is the blackening
of stone by fossil fuel, the slow burn
of loss and anger.

The weight of the past
seems to pin this city down.

Yet even in Lent,
the time of trial, silver threads weave
through the purple of mourning, sewing hope:
a peace trail, and the unseen paths of the many
who care. I find a house for asylum-seekers,
an Open Doors kitchen:

spots where the silver
deepens to a star.

                              When Yorkshire worsted
twines with Asian silks, Bradford defies
the gravity of history; its communities
refuse to be dragged down. In this altar-cloth,
above the dark strokes which depict the city,
above the rigid grid,

                                              a silver cell

breaks down in arcs of light.

                                  I think how the Spirit
is imagined as a bird, or as a flow
of living water in a dry land;
I think how it weaves through this tough place to lighten
and lift hearts. It is like that flight of geese
rising from the grey roofs,

                              like the stream of silver
which arcs through the Mirror Pool.

# Stitching the Long Kneeler

Skipton Pudsey Birkenshaw Rotherham Keighley
Oldfield by bus by car by foot by train Oakworth

        Three frames
in the ambulatory. Long canvas stretches
with the powerful colours of the four Church seasons
reduced to a pale hint, with faint outlines
to guide the sewing. For Rhona, partially sighted,
it is a blurred touchscape she can negotiate
only through the group's support.

        Three new members
in a three-year-old group that has steadily swelled
but fluctuates: here is Susan, who changed
her work hours to stitch, and here is Heather,
absent two years to care for her husband,
left with grief and a fridge tailored to his needs
she 'didn't recognise'. Returning a widow,
she was folded in friendship. Marjorie says
'We are being stitched together.'

        Stories are sewn
into the kneeler: a grandchild's birth, a niece;
a return soon after breast surgery; the news
of a death absorbed by all. Stories proclaim
rich identities: I meet Maria,
Portuguese-born, who stopped in Angola
in her move from South Africa. While a needle
is threaded with gold, a life moment
might be recounted. One was a bride
here on a New Year's Day, and asked for the bells

to peal at twelve, even if they split the skulls
of booze-befuddled sleepers.

                    I pick up the needle, scrutinise
the guiding holes in the weave, the untidy ends
on the reverse, waiting to be over-sewn.
Time concentrates to a needlepoint,
the worrying mind is no more than the precise homing
of steel into tiny hole which guides the entry
through stiff-resisting cloth, the long pulling through
of thread by freed needle, the desire
to make another diagonal stitch and then
another, the longing to flesh out
a tiny fragment.

Marguerite Barbara Jane David Jill Ann Barbara
Rhona Elsie Christine Ellie Patsy Maria Jean Susan
Pat Dianne Heather Marjorie Sue

                       The names
continue like the stitches; just add
a Greek Orthodox priest; then introduce children
now three years older; pull in visitors
from all over the world. Every name
is recorded in a book but each sewn mark
is proudly anonymous. 'This will outlast us.'

                    Tuesday after Tuesday
sustained by cups of tea, urged on by the stretches
of unworked canvas, by a still unsewn
harvest of luminous forms, week after week
the Stitchers return.

                     O true practitioners
of the spiritual life which is not so much a sudden
dramatic revelation or a gallery
of master-pieces boldly self-created;

but rather is the day-by-day returning
to a known place; it is the persisting
in a shared journey and each tiny effort
carries us one step after patient
step through unknown terrain
whose larger shapes we sense as implicit,
and yet can only glimpse:

                With that final stitch
the Stitching group will suddenly turn from ants
into kestrels. They will see the green
that is ordinary life, shot with the purple
of trial; they will pick out the patches
of intense red, and glory in the gold
that sings festival

              as the worked creation
stretches before them, patiently made whole.

# Unwilling Pilgrims

We are all displaced migrants
forced to journey
into the unknown:
even if we bolt the doors, pull down the blinds
of our safe houses, watch as they stale
into museums, all the while the city
is changing around us.

Pilgrims journeying
without a landmark: even if we have not left
faraway hot lands and risked oceans,
we find ourselves surrounded by new shop-fronts,
and motorways which bulldoze through our memories.
All around, the city turns to us
a stranger's face.

And walking at our side
are people whose skin colour, customs, dress
are unfamiliar, and suggest long journeys.
Strangers turn to friends, and friends drop
out of our lives, but the bonds and strains of travel
will either close
or break open our hearts.

Absurd pilgrims
who are weighed to the mud with costly luggage,
who tread an unpredictable terrain
in fashions which belonged to a safe haven.
Sometimes I face the future with opinions
that are 1960s mini-skirts. We all
peer at misleading maps.

At times our hearts
will be light and open as a pilgrim's scrip
which had no fastenings, held little more
than coins, an underwear change, a bowl and spoon.
At other times the harshness of the terrain
will force us to accept the alms of friendship
from a total stranger.

And the joy we expected
at our journey's end might suddenly brim inside us,
a table laid for us in the very midst
of hostile land. Had we stuck at home
we would have missed it. Whether or not we speak
of the kingdom of heaven, it is here
as an unexpected gift.

# Emily: Heretic or Mystic?*

## I

Marooned and motherless, she turned
Her loneliness to a gift:
She walked, and found a living God
In torrent, rock and drift.

She and her sisters showed their world
Its perfectly groomed face
As viewed by those kicked down in the dirt,
Those deemed a lower race.

Dead sisters, brother blundering in
Dead drunk, a mess of mud;
Behind the pub, a slaughterhouse
Which ran with animal blood.

Her world was fierce and uncontrolled;
Her God was too immense
To be contained by judging mouths,
Church walls, or common sense.

Out in the moor were rocks re-formed
By bullet-storms of hail;
Bent thorns forever forced to sculpt
The fury of a gale.

---

*\* Title of an event in the Bradford Literature Festival 2018.*

It was the storehouse of her mind;
Its heights and depths sufficed:
Whilst too many churchgoers failed to grasp
The passion that was Christ.

This woman had a wilderness soul;
She strode from soft delights.
Her heaven would be reached through hell
In a house called Wuthering Heights.

**2**

This story is founded on rock. At its fierce heart
Is a boulder-strewn expanse, and the house of stone
Which is its outcrop. This is the arena
Where each soul is tested. Blizzard-swept,
The moor becomes a white sea which drowns
Its row of sign-stones.

                                Just two miles away,
Another house, wadded with crimson carpet,
With library, chandelier and fluffy pet,
Its newer wealth protected by a bulldog
And legal deeds.

                                  To cross this distance
Is to risk the self. It is to cross a wilderness
Where moral markers vanish.

                                  The moor expels
Those fashioned by society, like a woman
Rushing from the Heights, in flight over snowy drifts
In her girl's silk dress, then gasping out her story
While a carriage waits by the Grange, while she is bound
For the garrulous huddle of London.

The protagonists:
                                  a woman who migrates
To that second house, and so commits herself
To a velvet-padded cell.
                                  a dark-skinned boy
Beaten, enslaved, who as a man returns
To exact a retribution more exacting
Than any scriptural law, who visits sins
With violence on the next generation,
Using the oppressor's tools: superior wealth,
And grasping legal deeds.

                              And a strange dream:
Sins never before imagined, multiplying
Like maggots, bloating out, and each one fleshed
To its separate life within a long sermon:
Seventy times seven sins:* the number used.

By Christ to explode arithmetic, to expand
The heart towards an infinite forgiveness,
Here is wearingly counted, sin added
To graphic sin, in a gloating inventory
Of trangressions.

                              The dreamer has a guide
Who escorts him from the Heights to this packed chapel;
Joseph, the cursing servant who spreads gloom
In the name of God. And as the preacher moves
To the four hundred and ninety-first sin, the one
Which cannot be forgiven, as accusations
Turn into blows, dream becomes a haunting:
Cathy's ghost is tapping at the window
Begging to be let in.

                              Elsewhere Emily wrote
Of God's embracing mercy that contains
The workings of justice. But how
Can this over-arching vision be played out
In such a harsh arena?

---

* *Then came Peter to him, and said, Lord, how oft shall my
brother sin against me, and I forgive him? till seven times? Jesus
saith unto him, I say not unto thee, Until seven times: but, until
seventy times seven. (Matthew 18.21–22)*

                                        An icy winter
Grips the lives of the younger pair; abused
And disinherited, the second Cathy
And Hareton slowly blossom into love
In tune with a spring-washed moor; they reconcile
The two houses.

                              But if theirs is the path
Of Christian forgiveness, what can we say
Of that dangerous passionate pair? Destructive
And self-destroying, haunting and haunted:
When death divides them, one is demon-driven,
The other a restless ghost.

                                        The writer throws
Her challenge straight at those of us who praise
Christ's radical forgiveness, judged in its time
A scandal and a blasphemy.

                                              We return
To the rock of the moor, an echo of the rock
Of eternity. This is the medium
Of Cathy's passion: necessary, bare:
Rock that endures, rock which outlasts the frippery
Of the flailing leaves above. After they suffer
Their separate hells, the lovers are released
Into the moor, to the freedom of its rock
And vast sweeps of space, the only heaven
That Cathy ever wanted.

                                        So is Emily
A heretic or mystic? To ask this question
Is to engage with justice and forgiveness:
It is to engage with Christ.

# A Mill Worker's Bank Holiday

A day for free. Release from limbs driven
Like machine pistons. Holiday from a skull
Turned to vibrating sound box by loom-din.

Setting off in twos, with swinging arms,
With exaggerated heel-to-toe strides,
As proper walkers do, as if now driven
By a machine called Exercise. But just suppose

one wandered from the road, feeling his feet
spring in sheep-nibbled grass,
feeling them adjust
to dip and rise and tangle,

letting his body
breathe in the silence,
re-attune
to the shimmer of birdsong.

Perhaps he stared
at rocks like rough-hewn altars, each hollowed
by a tiny rain-pool
holding in its mirror

a fragment of sky.
When in blurred dusk
He returned to the valley of murk, when the grime worked
Back into skin, when too soon the machine

Grabbed and shuttled his body like a bale
Of unresisting fleece, did his mind view
This trapped labouring self as if from afar?

Did part of his being still reside

out among rocks and sky?

# Titus Salt

A silent man.
A heavy schoolboy, struggling to relate,
judged indecisive. But the young man saw
how Bradford Beck flowed sewage, and how cramped
and ill the people were, how black poison
seeped into their lungs.

A Sunday school official, too timid
to read out the prayers, he held his peace;
and when he prayed aloud it was in rock
and flowing water: Yorkshire sandstone raised
to house a mill community; water piped
clean to each worker's house.

A man who still has words
thrust into his mouth, even by tea-towels
inventing Rules for his Saltaire. And yet
his deeds were bold: an industrial village built
in Italianate style, a chandelier-lit church
with large plain windows.

His legacy: a Victorian posed photo
of bulging waistcoat, bushy face; a line
of baffled historians trying to guess
his unspoken motives. He left a place
where art, not cloth, is weaving vibrant colours;
a place of holiday.

                    A gift transformed
beyond the imagination of the giver.

# Saltaire: A Story in Colours

Who would have thought
That white wool which laboured for long
In drab worsted
Suddenly should drape
Ladies in aniline mauve, that it should sweep
In strident green
Through gas-lit drawing rooms.

Who would have guessed
That sand-yellow stone
Would fight its own earth-pull, learn to climb
And over-hang, or that it would create
Its own tonal range: creased dark in shade,
Sullen in rain, or lit by the summer sun
To honey ochre.

Who would have known
This place of heavy dark
Looms would step us straight into the world
Of Hockney, to the Californian blue
Of a swimming pool, to spring bursting green
Through a Yorkshire road, making its asphalt bloom
A surprising magenta.

And through it all
The patient green of grass, the quiet mirror
Of a river once force-fed with violent dyes,
And now again transparent.
The towpath's grey is picked out by a flash
Of Asian pink. The tourist barge is a slab
Of steady red

Beside the stone bridge.
While down below
Runs the canal, a stretching looking-glass world,
Which de-constructs this boat
To a force-field
Of dips and ripples, hot vermilion pulsed
Against a sky brought close.

# Bradford Pals

*For the Cathedral members of the Bradford Pals regiment who died in the First World War.*

We might think about hands
Adept at kindling fires, surprisingly gentle
With a baby sister. Hands now purple-bruised
With hoisting heavy wood to prop the trench;
Hands that pick out lice, hands shrapnel-scarred;
Hands trained in the bayonet's lethal lunge, the deadly
Mechanics of guns.

You might think about feet
That strolled Market Street to meet the girls,
Feet that on arrival pranced with joy
What a lark to be in France! Feet now clogged
With sucking mud, feet frozen blotchy-red;
Feet dragged step after step on a night march
By an automaton body.

I might think about eyes
Whose work was to watch mechanised teeth combing
Wool into straightened fibres; eyes that saw
Their work transformed to the finest worsted cloth;
Eyes that ache with the unrelenting view
Of shapeless mud, eyes blinded by the flash
Of exploding shells.

Best not to think of minds
Divided, baffled: three of them were fighting
The country of their grandparents; all misled
By the promise of quick victory. That confusion

They took to the moment of death, running exposed
Not through the expected emptiness, but through bullets
Towards a waiting enemy.

Above all, best not to reverse
That image, cross the lines to clothe the soldiers
In field grey, and focus on a teenager
From Little Germany, one who chose to fight
For the land of his grandfather. Best not see him,
Also shivering, face his Bradford pals
Across No Man's Land.

# For Joe Hardcastle

*The bell-ringer Joe Hardcastle initiated an appeal to replace the Cathedral bells, which were declared unsafe in 1919.*

That morning Bradford woke to something wrong.
Something was missing. The ringers knew
Their bells were hanging lifeless: copper tongues
Each stiff, the huge mouths paralysed. They too

Were voiceless. Although too old for the dangers
Of war, they had tolled out their fallen friends.
Throughout the grisly fight they had rung the changes
Of hope, and now they saw their labours end

In a silenced peace. The autumn air was grey.
It sealed them in a vacuum, now no sound
Was travelling out in prayer. One man that day
Vowed to resist. Already in his mind

Bright notes flowed through the streets. Bell after bell
Pealed out for peace, befriended those who fell.

# There But Not There

*On Remembrance Day 2018, perspex silhouettes of First World War Soldiers were attached to the Cathedral chairs, in a country-wide initiative entitled There But Not There.*

At first you don't see it.
A glimpse, and it disappears. As your body
Bobs and dips through space, you catch it seated

On a chair beside a boy. Suddenly this gleam
Of a human frame translates into nothing
But the heavy oak behind.

It joins the unknown
Ranks of the poor who once crammed through the air
Suspended from the two side aisles where galleries

Jutted high. Two thrusts of storied space,
Now marked by an irregularity of stone,
A memorial no-one sees.

The feast of All Souls
Is a photo-negative in reverse: the living
Surrender their primacy, choose to dim,

So that for one November day the dead
Shape and light the foreground.

Nine days on,
Remembrance focusses on the silhouette
Of a dead soldier. You have it in your sight.

Now get your camera; trap and fix its image.
It is best approached obliquely: even then

Human technology struggles to focus

on something which is there but not there.

# Invisible Pathways

If the sun does not glint on its silver, you might miss
A snail's journey written across your step;
That hole burrowing under your fence is a clue
To the dig of claws, the white stretching of belly

That makes the path of a fox. High in the air
Is a criss-cross of wings, millennia of birds
Making their flight-paths over the routed city.
Already your human mind-map is opening out,

Losing its self-centre. In Buttershaw,
Alone in a bedroom, a girl rolls back her journey,
Undoes the jolting continents, nauseous seas,
To reach a Syrian home which may not now

Exist, but her heart is trekking that distance,
Longing to return. You trek those miles with her.
You live the bleak geography of loss.
Now look out beyond Bradford into the darkness

Which stretches over dale, out over sea
And foreign landmass. Watch how it crackles
With human tracks: hot anger texted
To a son in London; a Facebooked grandchild

Beamed straight to Pakistan; a tale of war
Emailed from Somalia. Dark space
Is a force-field of routes, a red-hot mapping
Of human connexions. Now you are attuned,

You might feel that the prayer breathed in this city
Is an act of travel, a quiet setting out
Beyond the known, the journey of a blessing
Heart towards the prayed-for. Or perhaps

You stick to known routes, keep an internal
Satnav racing you past a people-blur,
Turning others to obstructions, turning you
To a blind thrust towards a pre-set goal.

# Hidden Stories

I

The buildings hide their stories:
Look high above your head. This church carries scars
From the Civil War; its tower still feels the weight
Of protecting woolpacks

Hung from its battlement
Like stuffed stage bellies. Watch this one explode
In a sneeze of white fluff; and now watch
Cannon-balls crash

One. Two.
Then wander through this city: stories are written
Into its very fabric, histories hidden
Behind stone facades.

Deserted steps which lead to an architraved door
In Parkfield Road once bore the tired feet
Of journey-dazed children, just arrived
From the kindertransport;

Soon the sparse contents
Of tiny suitcases were spilt on beds;
Manila tags with identifying numbers
Were thrown away

At last. That night each child
Relived their last glimpse of parents waving
From the long platform, faces stretched to a smile;
And gripped that image with a tenacity

That might well have to last a lifetime.
Here are stories
Of war and exile; here too are stories
Of sheer dancing joy.

A palatial building
Is raining inside, yet its marbled dome
Once sheltered dancing feet, the throb and screams
Of a Beatles concert;

The air is dank
And thick with plaster-dust, but it remembers
Sudden darkness, pierced with a shaft of light,
Fred Astaire beamed straight

To this northern city,
To rows of wondering eyes.
This building was a story-book which turned
A new page every week.

**2**

When we are in church
We tell stories.

We tell of a people
Labouring in exile, struggling through the wilderness
To free themselves from oppression;

We tell of a king
Beautiful as any film star, who danced
In front of the Ark half-naked, hailed by trumpets,
And was condemned by a spiteful tongue
As vulgar.

And we tell of one whose stories
Still tease closed minds into a danger zone;
Who plants a seed of heaven into the earth
Of a simple story; one whose every act
Aligns him with the poor, the untouchables,
Confronts imperial power.

But we are not stuck
Antiquarians blindly burrowing
Through Iron Age tales:

We believe that a voice
Powerful as a Hebrew prophet might speak justice
From the margins of Bradford;

We look out
For an unexpected dance. We clear our throats
To sing a new song.

And we look for Christ
In everyone we meet.

One last story:
Hidden, because unmentioned in the press,
Buried in a scholarly paper. An old lady
Living near White Abbey Road, alone when the dark
Outside her curtains flares red and seethes
With shouts of riot. To her each yell is a missile
Striking into her home. All through that night
A young Muslim couple sit beside her,
Quietly talking, changing that small flat
From imagined target to a sanctuary:
A hidden place of hope.

# Before Pilate

There were two ways to kill him.
The first was easy: they had done that already
To thousands of others, but first
They dressed him in the purple robe of Rome,

And Pilate said,
'Years after your death we will embrace you,
And our embrace is lethal. You will see
The leaders of your Church strut in the robes

Of this Empire that condemns you to death.
We will make your name a battle-cry,
A shout for land and power, which will lead
Soldiers just like these to brutal wars.

And by the way,
Do not think you can escape this by dying
Between two outcasts. You will watch us load
Your priests with gold, and see them clutch and clutch.'

They all grinned,
Yes, that would finish him off more surely
Than any spear-thrust. Pilate drew close.
Now, earthly king, enjoy your crown of thorns.'

He stood alone
Dressed in that violent robe, its imperial purple
Streaked with innocent blood. The soldiers bowed
To their new master. No wonder

That grave could never be still.

# The Woman with the Spice Jar

Afterwards she would never know
whether that staringly public scene was the only
time she possessed him, or an act
of loss.

Yes, of course that moment tasted
of his flesh hot
and gritted from the road
(Their host hadn't even brought water).
And the salt
of his sweat – or was it
the salt of her own tears? -
all tousled together with her hair,

and that perfume heady
as a love-song,
filling her mouth, her kisses; pouring reckless
over his ankles, feet, the dirty floor;
gentling that room stacked with sour faces
into a bridal chamber,
even as her sobs

were tearing at the air, as if
they came from another throat.
And she thought she remembered
clutching his feet close between her breasts
trying to protect,
because now that ointment was smelling of a corpse
stretched out,
waiting to be embalmed.

**2**

She comes bearing Diprobase
which must be smeared generously on his body
to prevent bed sores.

She offers crushed

paracetemol (repeat prescription),
enalapril. She brings a bowl of water,

towels him dry.

She is constantly in contact with his body.
And when her thin hand

comes to rest

on his right arm, the one that can still feel,
that gesture holds

all those nights when their flesh

poured over and into each other. Now she holds him
knowing he is already half lost.

Now she pours

herself out in alarm-clocked startings awake
at 2 a.m.

when she sleep-walks to change his pad.
In his last days those carer's tasks
become an anointing.

# Women at the Tomb

They sat down, because their traumatised bodies
Had to sink to the ground. They sat and watched
That last straining act
Of rolling the boulder in place.

Nearby, blood
Dried on ungiving stone. Sleep was soured
With the hangover taste of too much shouting,
Too much death.

Their anointing jars held
The grief of the widows of the night arrest,
Of all who wait by prison gates and plead
For the location of a grave.

Their prayer was a track
Of longing that could only shock and bruise
Against the stone block,
And while other disciples

Were fleeing, rushing
To and from the tomb, trying to escape
Themselves,
Those women stayed present.

It was as if in a place where bombs
Had spat stones and slithered bricks, there remained
A stretch of path still pointing
To a disappeared home.

They prayed with a love that survived
Hope. Within that caving darkness time itself
Pivoted
And that prayer

Became the highway
By which he returned to an earth baptised
In dew, returned to encounter a woman's
Seeking.

# Mary of Magdala

The rooms felt more like wall than space;
The girl grew up confined
By heavy stone, and lattice made
The peephole windows blind.

Outside, dead fish dried out on wood;
This was Magdala's trade.
But in the lake, the living fish
Leapt in the light and played.

They sent her to the roof to spin;
Below, in a bowl of hill,
A new and shimmering element stretched,
Dynamically still,

Calming her turbulent waves of thought;
There deep called out to deep:
A shout, rebuke, and she was sent
Down into stone to sweep.

Her future loomed, a barricade
Of interlocking walls;
Defining her as task-doer, wife,
Mother – and that was all.

She knew this town of drying fish
And sightless rooms would hold
Her safe from even her deepest self:
Each hour would be controlled.

She snapped her thread, walked out alone,
She fought her prescribed role.
They said the seven demons ruled
Her wicked Godless soul.

He came, holding the stillness of deep
Water in his eyes.
He turned the roles that power constructs
To an absurd disguise.

Her seven demons he transformed
Into an angel band;
They set her free: her very self
Became an unexplored land,

Became a depth she could not plumb.
Then at his side she trod
The dusty tracks, and marvelled how
He found a glimpse of God

In leper, soldier, widow, mute,
And gave it back as gift
And challenge, to create a heaven
Within this world of rift.

And when they stretched him on the wood,
Dried out with thirst and pain,
She knew that hideous cross would rear
Endlessly in her brain,

Would block each vista, close each path,
Would mock her brief escape;
Her demons dared her not to hate,
Flaunting that torture-shape.

They rolled a rock to seal his tomb
Grief cut her like a knife.

Then a man who bore the marks of death
Did something strange to her life.

No court would hear a woman's word;
Her place was home and well:
And yet he told her, 'Do not cling
To me, but go and tell.'

And very soon the doubting men
Experienced what she said:
While Roman troops policed the streets,
The subversive whispers spread:

Her message trickled underground;
It surged with river force:
She knew what living water is:
She had stood at its very source

When waiting by a hopeless grave
Choked up with rock and shame
She heard a dead friend turned to living
Stranger speak her name.

# Dietrich Bonhoeffer

## 1 *In Bradford*

Does anyone notice him at Forster Square?
That blonde bespectacled German, who chose
To uproot himself, live 'unobtrusively'
As a pastor in London. This, he claims,
Will be his spell in the wilderness. A porter
Rushes past with a stack of leather cases.
He passes opulent shops, thin cloth-capped men,
A large newspaper hoarding which appears
To refer to football. (Have they even heard
The name of the Fuehrer?) There is City Hall
With its bold palatial Gothic. Now he reaches
A church of sullen sandstone, a small circle
Of grave German faces.

                                      He leaves
With the Bradford Declaration, a defiance
Of the Reich Church, of its vicious Aryan clause,
And the mounting pressure to deracinate
Jesus the Jew by shearing from the Bible
The Hebrew scriptures. This declaration
Bound for Berlin, is signed by all six pastors.

But as he waits to board the London train,
Holding this challenge to Hitler, do the words
Of another paper missive storm his mind
Like shock-troopers? Words written in a letter
From his friend Karl Barth, words which turn all England
To a coward's hideaway.

'return to your post
By the next ship . . . Your church's house is on fire.'
Then back to his Sydenham church. The re-introduction
Of Sunday school: the need to discuss its timing
With parents. The new pastor will organise
A nativity play. An appeal for more singers
To join his four-part choir. And can anyone bring
Flowers from time to time?

## 2 *The Wilderness*

Those were the hinge years: they were the pivot
On which his life swung: Bradford and London,
America, Norway, Sweden. Fighting the Reich
With conference speeches, running up phone bills;
Fighting, but from a distance. In due time
The wilderness would find him.

Before, a heavily freighted childhood. Ancestors
Of impressive worth, a house with coat of arms,
Old family portraits whose very frames
Spawned figures, foliage. Very soon the youth
Acquired the weight of expectation: doctorate,
Wadding of solid rank, distracting clutter
Of high opinions. And the moral burden
Of these substantial gifts.

After: a steady shedding: losing even
The thing he most believed he could control:
His moral purity. Undercover agent,
Pastor who bore the knowledge of a plot
To kill Hitler. 'On our blood
Lies heavy guilt.' Arrested, cast in prison,
Faced with new decisions. Did you use
Blankets whose sickening stench forced you to gag?
Or did you suffer cold?

                                    He surrendered
All hope of living months before his sentence,
Existing in near-death. Each shedding cleared
A space that God could permeate. This presence
He translated into writings; words buzzed
Out of that cell like hurrying messengers.

With his final loss, he moved beyond
The scope of human words, trusting in grace.
Stripped naked, led to be strung up;
Left in the end without even a body:
His bones reduced to incinerated ash,
Or slung in a mass grave, crumbling to dust:

Still out of dust a new world can be formed.

# Icons of the Spirit

## 1 *Writing an Icon*

We are told that an icon
is 'written', that each holy figure
is scripted by a centuries-long tradition
and birthed by prayer.

Then what can I call my act
of working with words? An improvised sketch?
A collage of Bradford-bits, a flurry
of impressionist daubs?

Words as brushstrokes
marking the blank page, hoping to surround
my tiny print-blocks with a white emptiness
quivering

like the air above a flame
with unseen presence.
Words which might draw
on dark shadows,

which might scrawl the muddle
of being human, and from this begin
to construct a still life
which is a prayer.

## 2 *Icon of the Holy Spirit*

*An icon in Bradford Cathedral's Chapel of the Holy Spirit.*

God-appearance held in a disc of wood:
A Spirit-hurricane laid out in gold,
pigments and egg yolk; laid out in calm
geometry. A white dove hovers

above Yorkshire rocks; twelve tongues of flame
hang neatly spaced inside the upper room
where twelve men sit in haloed clarity.
Circle-perfection.

I find myself reaching
for Rembrandt's brush,
for shadows so fierce they turn to fissures
cracking our smooth world-surfaces, gaping

into an ugly pit.
The rocks are here in the city.
Close to the Cathedral
rears a flat-block,

a sheer yellow cliff from which a mother
threw her child,
claiming to hear God's voice.
Numb despair

lived in that upper room like a beast of prey
savaging woman and man alike
after Jesus's bloodied body
was laid out on rock.

I reach for dark charcoal, stabbed and smudged
with clenched fist;
or if it must be paint, let it be oils
thick-daubed, grey-tinged,

because the woman I choose is tired.
Tired and tried. One bag holds potatoes
that must be peeled by six; another bulges
with husband's repaired laptop, heart pills

for house-bound neighbour, so many items
that will flow out in comfort
now drag
her arms with dead weight.

And home means conflict:
trying to explain
daughter's ecological zeal, which co-exists
with an untidy room, discreet tattoo,

to a father whose religious faith has retreated
to pronouncements learnt at school.
Trying to translate
the spirit-language of two different times

and generations,
trying to release
love locked away even from its owner's sight:
living in a no-man's land,

attacked from each side:
and all the while the body of a son killed
by a drunk driver
lying stone-cold

and motionless in her mind, blocking the way
to the God of her childhood prayers.

And while her husband vents his anger
on those around him,

she is impelled to travel
the pain of others, her only way
to protest at this unfair world. Sometimes she glimpses
a different God.

The mobile trills
like a summoning angel. Elderly neighbour
rushed to hospital. Neighbour's son
'tied up'. She steps into snow

blasted neon-red
by a curry-house front. Briefly she trudges
through slow-descending
blossoms of fire.

# Laying Down a Prayer-Mat

It's those two sculptures
which stop you in your tracks
and then you notice
the railways lines which once powered north
and London-wards, their ends not quite meeting.
This is the remains
of the old Forster Square,
proud station of a wool-powered city;
now each track-end
is a rhythmic twisting-upwards and leaning-together
of steel, and between the two sculptures,
a paved space.

That stretch of wall
seems green-moulded, and the old arcade
repeats its steady curves. It walls in
the long-disappeared presence
of a hooting, hurried, steam-belching station.
This heavy arching
of grey stone subverts our sense of time
as if this might be any ancient city,
even Jerusalem.

Monks vowed to poverty
at Lindisfarne once carried prayer-mats
protecting them from a dirty kneeling-place;
through this mat they rooted inward stillness
in a particular spot.
Now throughout this city, Muslim worshippers
lay down their prayer rugs,
daily companions
on journeys, on the Hajj pilgrimage.

A homeless man stretches his stained blanket
under a stone arch; he rummages
in his broken-strapped bag for a Basics bun.
A young man strides past fashion-plated
in jeans with designer holes;
low down, those torn denims slumped
on a frayed blanket certainly do not signal
an ironic nod to a trend. This man's aura
is the smell of unwashed clothes; it is a zone
of swivelled-forward heads.

People power past, their bodies pointed
In the track-direction;
this is now a route
for shoppers from Broadway, passengers
for the re-located station. Some are welded
hand and eye to mobiles whose removal
would feel like an amputation. They tread
where mill-owners boarded London-bound trains,
their minds finessing business deals, where porters
rushed with stacked trolleys, disappearing
down a Victorian-tiled passage, luggage-way
to the Midland Hotel.

Another man lays down the small sum
of what he owns in the cell of the next arch.

The prayer-mat tells us
that any place on this curving-away earth
might be holy ground
if we could only begin
to see differently.
It might a squeezed flat in Holme Wood,
or any shop or café where the currency
is more than money.
It is Valley Parade, whose roaring stands
and darting footballers play every game

beside a grey memorial that names
the dead of the fire.

But here
between two stalled rail-tracks which are both
end and journey-start
seems as good a place as any to isolate
a space of stillness, to create a clearing
in the midst of busyness
to weave a prayer
which takes in sweat-reek
and body-creased blanket, which embraces
the woman with a Primark carrier bag,
the Victorian navvy, the medieval friar
seeking alms;

                    and blesses this child
who is pirouetting in her new pink skirt
right in the middle of the sculptures.

# Billy Liar

A teenager stuck in an early 60's world
of black and white. A dreamer trapped
in the monochrome sludge of film. A funeral clerk.
He still lives at home, where he is coffined
in narrow custom.

                                        In Undercliffe
he tries and fails to feel a girl's warm flesh.
Gaunt gravestones rear like spectres. He escapes
in fantasies. The armies of Ambrosia
march through his mind and uniform him in power.

We need to throw some colour at the screen:
some Asian reds and golds. We need flat water
to rise in fireworks, make the night explode
in jewel-fountains at the city's heart.

We need to fast-forward to a Bradford
where even the eatery names fly into dreams;
Sultan, Mystic Pizza. Push our hero
to the museum where imaginings
swell and flicker across a blank
huge rectangle. We need to make him rap,
upload a quirky video, slam a poem.

Now he would not bottle it, and flee
from the London train, or even need to approach
a Bradford station. The story would not end
with a defeated Billy walking home
at the head of his fantasy band. Now he would stride
triumphant through this City of Film,
and be followed by a twitter feed.

# Reflections for the
# September Equinox

This is the moment
when sun-fire wheels perpendicular
to tilt of earth, when air becomes a medium
of gold light, when night and day are held
in circling-past balance:

we might read
the dales as patiently as this breath of wind
lingering on tree-tops, fingering
the braille of the landscape;

we might notice clouds
poised above the dale like fat brush-heads
loaded with shadow. Impelled to sweep
through a wash of green-gold, they saturate
a clump of trees in black;

we might rejoice
with apples slow-rounded to red
globes, clustering almost incongruous
along a gnarled branch;
completed, yet hanging by a stalk
between their long summer-swell and a loosening
jolt to earth;

we might attend
to the starvation of trees, whose leaves begin
to brittle back to vein, breaking down
their own chlorophyll, with the unseen bleeding
of its remnant back to twig;

yet they convert
their wounds to gold: at times the tree pretends
to be a splash of sunlight

as it moves
towards a shedding like a relief:
a trunk rising bare from a scattering
undress of leaves,
a tree which seems to step out of the garment
which was its former self.

# Fellow-Travellers

it plunges
away from our straining eyes:
a vanished quiver
of tail, scale-flash, quick-
silver streak of minnow
appearing
to make solid
the properties of water
for a blink of a moment, separated
from the viewer by a gasp-line of air,
a surface-ripple;
both of us know
to cross that line is death.

we might have missed
the life beating high above our heads,
those greylag geese
flying a spaced track of dark earth-stuff
across the blue of space
powering air-strokes
through a region barred
to our lumbering human frames
unless we are cased
in ponderous machines

this native harebell
hides itself
within a tiny seed and lives slow
winter made out of claggy earth,
suffers a dank smothering that mimics
our human burial

yet it translates
the cold cling of mud
to petals which are membranes of light

and stranger still
all things of earth are fashioned from the dust
of long-dead stars: we share the imprint
of radioactive blaze, life-shrivelling cold
and airless sterile rock: all this is encoded
in skin, blood and spittle
and it lives
in tail, wing and gill.

This is the very DNA
of our longing.
we hold in our bodies
the beating lived moment and the code
of all that is outside it, all that lives
and signals death to us:
our bodies hold a lineage of black holes
even as we laugh or chatter.

our companions
creatures of the flood and air-path,
the plants of heavy earth,
the persistent presence
of insect, bird, of cloud and reaching tree
which are both kin and stranger:
gifting us
with the surprise of scales, of feather, fur,
sun's sculpting rays, beak's pitiless precision,
clawing of waves, rocks which hold millennia
in a few inches:

these our fellow-travellers
close but elusive, far homelier
than our notion of angels, more mysterious

than our colonising brains
dare to allow:

                                     powerful in presence,
yet undemanding, each one asserts
its otherness; they draw our imaginations
to reach outside the safe seal of skin,
the boundary of breath;
wordless, they lead us
to the silence of encounter:
this is an act
which some might call prayer.

# Voices From the Other Side

I was clear river passing through gill
and gobble-mouth. I was brown scale
and tail-flick. I cruised bubble-raising
though treed shadow, liquid stretch of sky.
I nosed silt-depth. I nibbled trailing green
and made it me. I dodged the clean death
of pike-bite. Now my river is an enemy
pushing deep inside me. Now it sludges
my guts dirt-purple. It clogs my gills
to air-gasp. It vomits me to the surface.
I am floating scum. I am culverted underground.

To make the cloth: machines to card, to comb
To slub, to twist; wool feeding row on row
Of roller-roar. To make the cash: get up
At six, cold splash, tea-gulp, run streets,
Sprint closing gates, start hours of brain-split noise,
Jam-sandwich-taste, back to machine, air-fluff.
Near eight, rush home. Bradford a choked room,
fug-ceilinged, murk-walled. I am fourteen.
My hair is blonde. I plait and tuck it back
so the machine won't claim a scalp. They say our cloth
is worn by fine ladies at the court.

You did not listen to those two other voices.
Why should you hear me cry from the near future
you think you will somehow dodge? Your poisonous dyes
shat into streams. Your giant chimneys smoked
as if addicted. You sold us progress.
I, who consumed little, am the first
to be swept away. The sea cannot scream.

Its mouth is choked with plastic. The land cannot shout.
It has become trashed sea. What was my island
struggles to stretch its last gasp of earth-throat,
its fast-drowning peak, above the waves.

Do not feel virtuous when you rescue me
in one of your big ships. Rather be warned
that tree, animal, bird, everything that makes
this bold, always fallible earth-experiment
Is almost beyond rescue. Pray with deeds.

# Prayer

You who are the new life
curled within me, however tired my hopes
however old my failures;

You who are the wisdom
in the smile of the Downs child to the stressed grownup
who thinks he is in control;

You who are the alms
outstretched in a beggar's hand, offered to the trader
who looks away, dropping his coins from a height;

You flare out of winter
in bursts of blossom, turn each one of us
to Moses silent by the burning bush;

Often you are a night landscape flowing
around a mean house with peephole windows
through which I see only dark,

But I can draw towards you in darkness
moving beyond the brain's electric brilliance
and entering silence.

My words stutter: my clearest images
bleach away. My thought-constructions
are shoddy temples

yet their crashed stones
might at least pave a broken path that points
towards a mystery
leading ever deeper
even as it eludes me

# Centenary: 25 November 1919

Antiques, Old Gold, Old Silver, Old False Teeth;
We struggle to get our bearings. H.M. Government
is advertising 'invalid cars on wheels'
in a list of surplus furniture. Discharged soldiers
plead for work, and the UK delegation
has asked for 'bomb throwing' to be removed
from the draft of the Belgian Olympics. We have surfaced
in 1919. We are straining our eyes
at the close-crammed print of Bradford's daily paper.

People jostle for attention: refined young lady
'who desires to meet steady young man'; a husband
who refused the billiard room to his wife's guests
because they would wear out the carpet, and the cry
'I am badly in need of Empty Bottles for Wines
and Spirits'. Then there is that sinister character
(at least to our eyes) like a Father Christmas
with an evil grin hidden behind his beard:
Bachelor (38) retired officer
wishes to 'UNCLE' JOLLY (gentleman's) children
Christmas holidays onwards, London district.

At the Palace theatre, a 'capital entertainer'
whose song expressed the feelings of 'even a negro'.
But in the 'desert acres' of war-shocked France
is a depot run by 'estimable ladies',
funded by Bradford Commerce. And hidden away
at the bottom of the last page: a dismissive rebuttal
of the claim that in the war the church failed.

And while a journalist frets that at Frizinghall,
the trolley arm of the trams is turned to reverse
by a long cane, four thousand miles away
in India, this year's events have moved
to non-violent protest, which will shape
the lives of future Bradford residents
and change the cityscape.

                              All of this held
in a Godspan of a moment.

                              And in London,
announced under the royal coat of arms
in the Gazette, the King's Most Excellent Majesty
grants Bradford a Cathedral.

                              Which is unnoticed
on the actual day in Bradford's Telegraph;
So Christ is born in the muddle of our lives
in the midst of coal shortages, deep suspicion
of 'German guile', toffee, and cures for bunions.
He appears just when we are focussed on an advert
for a hornless gramophone. He is born in the midst
of human and animal mess, hidden somewhere between
Lost: Astrachan Glove (right hand) and Found:
White Nanny Goat.

# Centenary: Icons of Bradford

City Hall: a shouting out of power
Fuelled by sheep; a wool trade so wealthy
It dares to copy a Venetian palace;
It challenges the sky. Here at the front
Is English history petrified in sandstone,
A line of kings and queens.

              When the local paper
Wrote about the royal decree that birthed
Bradford's Cathedral, its reporting style
Was dry official-speak of annual sum,
Procedures, population, benefices;
Columned statistics.

            Now at Bradford's heart,
beside the rearing rock of City Hall,
we find the element that gravitates
to the lowest places. Water reflecting
kaftans, pink chemises, tough jeans.
A teenager adjusting her hair
before she takes a selfie. A child's rucksack
badge-studded, trainers, hijabs all
kaleidoscoping.

              Bradford reflected
as fluid presence, made and remade.
A pool which plays, creates its own causeway
yet always holds the infinity of sky
here, at our feet.

The sandstone monarchs still reign in glory
from City Hall, but elsewhere the Victorious
fabric is flaking. Willowherb
rules on roofs; lordly banks mutate
to cut-price stores. The Rolls-Royces
that cruised Darley Street now haunt the memory
as ghost chariots parked outside Primark.

A vulnerable city: a Cathedral
once in financial shortfall; football club
twice in administration. Constant fires.
The Christian faith no longer rules, but then
Jesus chose at huge personal cost
never to rule that way.

                                    At the consecration
of the restored bells, the guides for the day
were Muslim schoolchildren, who told
surprising facts to elderly worshippers
about their own cathedral. And the bells
peeled out, in a sea-wave of sound
flowing through vacant air. A rich mix
of people who make Bradford joined a liturgy
of gratitude, and shared the child heaven
of squirty cream and strawberries.

A Mirror Pool supplied by Bradford Council
that offers baptism
in the joy of water

a small and far-from-rich Cathedral
offering to bless
every citizen by reflecting back
the Godself within them.

# I Am*

I am the night that lights the moon.
I am the words that mark the silence.

I am the lake that holds the clouds.
I am the rain that will be lake.

I am the bank that makes the river:
The river that creates the bank.

I am the church that shapes the stone:
The curve of space that is the bowl.

I am the hope that speaks the city.
I am the prayer that breathes the soul.

I am the sky that draws horizons;
The bite of air that firms the bridge.

I am the dance that moves the limbs.
I am the body that is the dance.

I am the mother that grows the child:
The baby's genes that live her forebears.

I am God that is. I am humankind
That births God into a place and time.

*A tribute to Charles Causley's 'I am the Song'.

# Seeing Christmas

A night so still
it seems to hold its breath;

The lone eye of a star
splitting the dark sky, piercing to earth
with the white heat of its gaze;

Sheep untended
on rocky hills, three life works of study
faltering at the last hurdle;

                                        Tough shepherds
and lauded sky-scholars both directed
to look anew;

Lumbering cows
and angels brought together into one
huge sweep of seeing;

Wheeling star
and earth-trampling oxen both focussed
on a tiny scrap of life.

Draw close.
The straw will muffle your footsteps; take your place
behind that dirty-foot shepherd:

Do not speak.
You have left your words behind; for just a moment
You eavesdrop on yourself.

All too soon
a camel will bellow, and its owner
will think of the long road back;

All too soon
a mobile will trill and you or I
remember some pressing task;

All too soon
the human mind will sever cows from angels,
turn nature into a tool;

And then the thugs of the power-mad king will advance
on this troublesome brat
popped up where you'd least expect;

But for just a moment
you glimpsed a new self, scarcely born
and still so frail,

threatened with violence
from the status-makers, from your own mask-selves,
and yet alive

in a God-depth of yourself,
struggling to survive, longing to look
out through your eyes to show you a different world.

# Angels of Bradford

If there are any angels
who might visit Bradford, it would be the three,
almost off-duty, who dropped in on Abraham
as humans, and were fed.

Here they would come in the guise
of kindertransport children, Asian workers,
Syrian refugees, Rohingya Muslims
and find a welcome, and each offer back
their own particular blessing;

                    in Holme Wood
a woman tries to sleep on a pillow of worries
and debts, hard as the stone on which Jacob
rested his travel-tired head. Her council flat
and each tough Bradford-place might be the foot
of a ladder flowing with angels;

                    Gabriel, Jibreel,
bless this city that proclaims the sacred
in the midst of disused mills.

                    Let women trust
their wings of longing and soar. Let men voice
the heaven-cry of a peace that seeks justice.
Let the child whose life is already closing in
like a dark tunnel glimpse a light-quiver
of possibility, an opening out
that may surprise with sky.

Seer of Patmos
who spoke of seven angels, each inhabiting
an Asian church, call into being the angel
of this cathedral, not with doom-trumpets
but with the voice of a chorister.

                                     Let it spread
huge-feathered wings over this hut of stone.
Let the song of wonder weave into its prayers
and seep into its silences. Angel-voice,
speaker of demanding truth, send out this church
to affirm the holy in what seems most broken.

May all who come here find both home and road.
May it be both angel-messenger and friend.